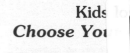
"I like it beca...

Robert Nucci, age 9

"I recommend these books because they make you read extraordinary things."

Daniel Hayes, age 8

"These books make you feel like you are making the life risking decisions, not reading about somebody making all of the choices as they write the book."

Matthew Fiaschetti, age 10

"I like *Choose Your Own Adventure* because it feels like you're actually in the real book."

Alexander Rivera, age 9

"I love these books because some are haunted and some are not. There are a bunch of adventures and there are a bunch of different endings. That is what I like about *Choose Your Own Adventure*."

Maddie Ryley, age 8

CHINESE DRAGONS

BY R. A. MONTGOMERY

ILLUSTRATED BY VLADIMIR SEMIONOV
COVER ILLUSTRATED BY JINTANAN DONPLOYPETCH

CHOOSECO
WAITSFIELD, VERMONT

Book design: Stacey Boyd, Big Eyedea Visual Design

For information regarding permission, write to:

CHOOSECO

P.O. Box 46, Waitsfield, Vermont 05673
www.cyoa.com

Publisher's Cataloging-In-Publication Data

Names: Montgomery, R. A. | Semionov, Vladimir, illustrator. | Donploypetch, J. (Jintanan), 1981- illustrator.
Title: Chinese dragons / by R.A. Montgomery ; illustrated by Vladimir Semionov ; cover illustrated by Jintanan Donploypetch.
Other Titles: Choose your own adventure ; 30.
Description: [Revised edition]. | Waitsfield, Vermont : Chooseco, [2009] | Originally published: New York : Bantam Books, ©1991. Choose your own adventure ; 109. | Summary: You are a young orphan in 7th century China. You've never had many options, but your bravery, wisdom, and skill may now open up doors for you in the dawn of the Tang Dynasty. Powerful warriors are bringing change all around you. Who will you become now that you are free from the drudgeries of servitude on your uncle's farm?
Identifiers: ISBN 1-933390-30-1 | ISBN 978-1-933390-30-7
Subjects: LCSH: Orphans--China--Juvenile fiction. | Outlaws--China--Juvenile fiction. | China--History--Tang dynasty, 618-907--Juvenile fiction. | CYAC: Orphans--China--Fiction. | Outlaws--China--Fiction. | China--History--Tang dynasty, 618-907--Fiction. | LCGFT: Action and adventure fiction. | Choose-your-own stories.
Classification: LCC PZ7.M7684 Ch 2009 | DDC [Fic]--dc23

Published simultaneously in the United States and Canada

Printed in Malaysia

10 9 8 7 6 5 4 3 2

For Ramsey. We miss you.

Special thanks to Torrey Paquette and Vlad Semionov for working hard to depict ancient China accurately and beautifully. – RM

BEWARE and WARNING!

This book is different from other books.

You and YOU ALONE are in charge of what happens in this story.

There are dangers, choices, adventures, and consequences. YOU must use all of your numerous talents and much of your enormous intelligence. The wrong decision could end in disaster—even death. But, don't despair. At any time, YOU can go back and make another choice, alter the path of your story, and change its result.

The year is 620 AD, the dawn of the Tang Dynasty in China. You live and work on your uncle's farm on the North China Plain, just south of the Yanshan Mountains and not far from the Yellow River. Your days toiling in the fields are long and arduous, and you often daydream of a more exciting life. One day, a group of Mongolian Turks invades your village, and you are taken prisoner. If you make a dash for freedom, you might be able to save your family. On the other hand, taking your chances as a prisoner might allow you to escape to a better life. The choice is yours!

The room where you sleep is small and cramped. In one corner the sacks of seed needed for planting are kept. There are not as many sacks as usual, and your uncle and his wife are worried. They have eleven mouths to feed and only a small patch of land upon which to earn their livelihood. Your uncle, Wei T'ai, is not a mean man, yet neither is he happy and easygoing. Life has been hard for him, and the opportunities that others readily take advantage of he has seldom taken. Consequently, the parcel of land left to him by his father, a man well loved in this small Chinese hamlet located outside the walls of the great town of Luoyang, has dwindled from a sizable piece that once commanded respect to a scraggly plot of land that now yields little, even in the best of times.

The dark part of the night has already passed, and the sky lightens slowly with the promise of sun and warmth. It has been a long and hard winter, fast on the heels of a fall when the harvest offered little. The old people in the village talk unhappily about the time of the great droughts when thousands of people died, and when those who could walked hundreds of miles to the south in search of food and work. Some of those travelers returned with grim stories of bandits, thieves, and murderers. They did not find food, work, or housing. And they were not welcome. The Great Mother Earth of China could be cruel, and the people feared those days. The Chinese Dragons, kindly spirits who brought the rain for the crops, were nowhere to be found.

Turn to page 2.

2

You shift in your bed, trying to find a soft spot. The mattress, made of leaves and wheat stalks, is hard and lumpy. The room is cold, and a persistent wind comes off the vast steppes of Inner Mongolia. It finds you wrapped in a thin, coarse hemp cloth blanket, your only guard against the cold.

Unable to sleep, you push the blanket aside, careful not to disturb the mongrel dog who shares your bed, and step onto the earthen floor that even in the summer is never warm. A window fashioned from greased paper and shuttered against the cold draws you toward it. The rusted iron catch yields to your touch, and you peer through, gazing out at the dawn.

The tinge of red in the sky is like a magic show to you, and your heart leaps, taking you far from the hardships of your life. Images of warmth, enormous banquets, clothing, and a farmhouse that would please a person of any taste all rush through your mind. They are quickly replaced with sadness, brought on by the sudden memory of your parents, who have long since succumbed to a disease that took many lives in your village.

Go on to the next page.

You leave off your feelings of sadness and the dreams that give you small comfort and turn back to the realities of your life. Today is to be a long day of work, preparing the fields for planting. Soon your uncle will call, and you like to be up and ready before then. These quiet moments are yours to be alone.

When the morning call comes, it is more like an alarm than a call to wake up and begin your day. You wish with all your heart that you were with your friends in your own village, and your parents were alive. But wishing will not make it so. Your life is here and now, and you have a day's work to do.

Turn to the next page.

4

"I'm coming! I'm coming!" you yell, slipping on your only pair of shoes. You leave the shed, cross the courtyard, and enter the main house where the rest of the family is gathering for breakfast.

"You are to do the field in the upper section. It must be ready by tomorrow," your uncle, Wei T'ai, says to you. Before you can reply he is talking to the others, giving your cousins their tasks for the day. The two oldest sons are the favorites of the family, and they get the easiest fields to cultivate. The daughters must also work in the field, breaking up the thick yellow earth to ready the soil for plantation. They work just as hard as the men, only they are never given recognition for it. They have your sympathy, and although you are not particularly close to them, you get along well. Your older, male cousins, on the other hand, don't like you. Even though you are family, to them you are an outsider and another mouth to feed. You are very careful to steer clear of them.

"I want more!" demands the eldest son, and he is given a generous ladle of gruel in his bowl. When one of the girls pushes her bowl forward for another portion, she is roughly rebuked, and the remaining ladle is poured into the father's bowl. You don't even bother to ask for a second helping.

Turn to page 9.

6

Reluctantly, you turn away from the road and the idea of attending the sacrifice. Your heart is heavy, and your feet are sluggish. The whole day of work spreads out before you. Black Moon senses your disgruntlement and tries his best to amuse you with his old tricks that have always been able to elicit a smile. Unable, even, to get your attention, he too looks wistfully at the road beyond the small family compound.

"Where did I leave my knife?" you ask out loud. Black Moon looks at you quizzically. You are sure that he understands all that you say. After all, he has been with you since he was a puppy, and together the two of you made the journey from your old house to your new life with your uncle.

"Ah, there it is," you say, picking it up and taking the small, clean blade from its sheath, which is carved from two thin pieces of willow. You are proud of the knife; it was a present from your father, and you tie it up carefully to your belt. "Let's go, Black Moon," you say, then head for the field where you are to work the earth.

The morning sun soon takes the chill out of the air, and the earth breaks apart under the force of the hoe. Sweat pours down your brow, and your hands, calloused from work, grasp the shaft. You imagine it being a lance, and yourself a warrior fighting under the command of the great Li Shi-min.

Suddenly the sky is filled with the flight of hundreds of arrows! A fierce shout from your uncle shudders through the otherwise calm morning air.

Go on to the next page.

"Run for the house! Run for your lives!" you hear, as the scream trails off. You are frozen to the spot as a dozen wooden-shafted arrows plant themselves around you like an instant forest at your feet. Miraculously, none of them have hit you. Looking up, you see hordes of angry-looking men on horses, their bright red and yellow banners flying, their lances and swords glinting in the sun. A cloud of dust follows behind them. The noise and shouting envelop you.

"Catch that one!" shouts a bearded man in a mixture of Chinese and the language of the Orkhon Turks. You recognize individual words— in your old village there lived a Mongolian Turk, a prisoner from a raid several years back who had been wounded and left to die. Your father took him in and treated him. Once recovered, the Turk became part of the village, even marrying a Chinese woman. His name was Ogot, and he always spoke of his displeasure toward all of the fighting and killing.

These men, however, are different. They are here to pillage and kill, to take livestock and what little food there is for themselves. Whatever is left they will burn. There is little or no mercy with these Turks of the Eastern Khanate. Their leader, the great khan Tu-Li, is feared throughout the regions of Inner and Outer Mongolia. It is against his warriors that Li Shi-min, the soldier hero of China, fights. It is against raids such as this that the sacrifice of the white horse is to be made today at the River Wei.

Turn to the next page.

8

Three horsemen surround you. They are wearing short woolen shirts with leather vests. Their baggy trousers are tucked into fur-covered boots. As the first one reaches for you, Black Moon leaps for his throat. With a swipe of his arm the horseman knocks Black Moon aside.

"I've got this one! You get the others," the man shouts. With a grin, he sweeps you up onto his horse.

"Let go!" you shout in his own language.

"What do we have here? More trouble than we want, it seems. Quiet or you'll end up like that dog of yours!" Black Moon, you realize, is still lying on the ground. He is unconscious and does not respond to your call.

You reach for your knife, but the Turk quickly grabs your wrist and stops you. Viciously he throws you to the ground, and you lie there stunned.

"So, you refuse to come along. Perhaps you would like to remain here, with the others?"

Turn to page 16.

"Have you heard about the sacrifice?" Shining Face, the middle daughter, asks. Everyone is silent for a moment. These are dangerous times in China. A sacrifice usually means trouble of some sort.

The year is A.D. 620, and China is in the throes of continuing internal struggle and attacks by the barbarian Eastern Turks all along the border of Mongolia. The Turks, with their savage cavalry, rush into the small towns and villages with their lances shining, their sabres cutting, and flights of arrows filling the air until the sun is almost obliterated. However, there is hope for China in the form of the Great Warrior—Li Shi-min.

Turn to page 11.

Li Shi-min is the son of Emperor Gaozu, and the soldier hero of China. He is young, but he is fearless, bright, and ambitious. Wherever he goes he commands the respect of both his own men and the enemy. With his own people he shares their hardships, living in the field, doing hand-to-hand combat, and never asking his men to do things that he himself would not do. His name fills people with pride and awe—as well as fear. For you, his name fills you with hope, and the chance to dream of a way out of this hard life that you have fallen into.

Turn to the next page.

12

"This sacrifice, is it for a battle to be fought or for a victory?" your uncle asks. You survey the faces at the long wooden table. His two sons are eager to hear, you can see it in their eyes.

"For a battle to come, Father," replies Shining Face.

"Then we must not rejoice. A battle means hard times, danger, death. Ours is but a field to be trampled upon. It does not matter by whom. They will destroy anything or anyone in their way."

"But, Father, a sacrifice! It is to be a white horse! Li Shi-min himself is to be there," Shining Face exclaims, excited at the prospects of the ritual.

"Where?" asks the youngest son, in a tone anything but friendly.

Go on to the next page.

"At the bridge over the River Wei, two hours from Luoyang," she replies. You feel a rush of excitement. *I must go,* you say to yourself. *I will go,* you promise.

"Enough of this talk," your uncle says. "One sure way for all of us to die is to not plant the fields. So, get to work. Let this warrior sacrifice his horse and his life if that's what he wants. We have work to do."

Turn to the next page.

14

You look at your cousins, then at your aunt and uncle. You rise, and your day begins. Silently you file outside into the courtyard, gather your hoes and spades, and head for the section of land assigned to you.

"I wish I could go to the sacrifice," you say out loud. Nobody hears you though, and you are thankful that they have not.

Your dog, black furred, short and powerful, nuzzles your hand. You forgot him this morning, and he reminds you of your duty to him.

Go on to the next page.

"I'm going to feed Black Moon," you yell. Your uncle nods, and you turn back to the courtyard where you pour water, soy, and rotting wheat grains into a rough bowl. As Black Moon eats, you gaze out toward the road that leads to the river and the place of the sacrifice. There are people on the road, and you are sure that they are on their way to see the great Li Shi-min.

You want to go to the sacrifice, but you wonder if you should risk your uncle's anger.

If you decide to go to the sacrifice,
turn to page 17.

If you decide to stay and work in the field,
turn to page 6.

16

You hear the screams of what sound like your uncle and cousins. But you can't be sure. You know that these barbarians delight in brutalizing their victims. You've heard stories, all too true you now realize, of skulls lain end to end, or found in piles throughout the land. They number in the thousands and lie bleached by the sun and rain, a testament to the power of the Chinese Dragons.

The screaming stops, and you know within your heart that the life has gone out of those who were once your family.

The Turk does not wait for your answer and rides off, certain that you are too frightened to run away, too stunned to even think.

You've got to do something, you realize. But what? A run for freedom could be risky. Perhaps it would be best to remain where you are and take your chances as a prisoner.

If you wait where you are, turn to page 21.

*If you make a dash for freedom,
turn to page 33.*

You wait until your uncle and cousins are out of sight, on their way to the fields with hoes and spades. You feel a tinge of excitement mixed with apprehension. You are already in bad with the family to begin with. Going to the sacrifice is sure to get you in even deeper trouble. But what do you have to lose? you reason. They treat you more like a servant than a relative anyway. What more could they do to you, especially if you never return?

"I'm my own person!" you say out loud, careful to keep your voice low. "Come, Black Moon," you tell your dog, who has been waiting patiently. He acknowledges your words with a nuzzle to your hand.

It doesn't take long for you to get out of sight of the farm. Once you are on the road, you feel fine. The sun warms your back through the poor cloth of your shirt, and your feet feel good as they hit the powdery yellow earth. You whistle the way you used to when you lived with your parents. Their memory brings sadness to you, but it soon passes as you concentrate on the adventure that lies ahead.

Turn to the next page.

"Hey, you there!" comes a voice. Looking up you see a middle-aged man and his wife heading in the same direction.

"Sir? Are you talking to me?" you ask.

"A brass coin says you're on your way to see the sacrifice. Another one says your parents don't know you're going." He laughs, but it is a kind laugh.

"Leave the youngster alone," his wife says. She has a friendly look to her face, and you take an instant liking to these two people.

"What village are you from?" you ask, falling into step alongside them.

"Oh, you wouldn't know it. It's a small place to the north of here. Right now we're on our way to Luoyang to find jobs, start a new life," he says. You like the sound of his voice. "We could use someone like you. Am I right that you've left home?" he asks.

"Well, you might say that." Briefly you tell them about your parents and the story of the plague that killed them. They are very sympathetic; you can see it in their faces and hear it in their voices.

Turn to page 20.

"I'm a tailor, my wife is a painter of fine pottery. We can use a helper. What do you say? Would you like to join us?" he asks, looking at you expectantly.

You are tempted to go with the couple. But you also wish to go to the sacrifice where you hope to find Li Shi-min and his army. The couple offers you an opportunity for security; Li Shi-min on the other hand, might offer you a position in his army.

If you decide to go with the couple,
turn to page 25.

If you decide to continue on your way to the
sacrifice, turn to page 35.

You decide that it is wiser to stay where you are. Smoke from the burning buildings stings your eyes and burns within you. You gag on the hot, thick air, lost and bewildered in the midst of this horror. *I knew I should have gone to the sacrifice*, you lament. Slowly tears of overwhelming sorrow mixed with rage flush your cheeks. This was your family. Now they too, like your mother and father, are gone. Once again you are thrown on the mercy of the world. It's been your experience that its mercy is far from generous. You kick your foot into the earth, trying to keep your mind off all the uncertainty that surrounds you.

Suddenly your instincts are on full alert. Something or someone is moving slowly and quietly nearby. For a moment the thick smoke clears, but you see no one. You are filled with fear, which is soon replaced with anger fueled by your desire for revenge. Your small knife, its blade as sharp as the day it was given to you, slips into your hand. You don't really know how to use the tool as a weapon, but you are guided by instinct.

Crouching, ready to defend yourself, you vow that you will not be taken easily. Like a cat, you slide toward the row of willow trees that divides your uncle's land from his neighbor's. Being in motion seems to cleanse you of fear, and your mind is keen and perceptive. You see everything clearly. You feel as if you can hear as well as a dog and move as fast as a ferret. Then you see it—a person close to the ground is coming toward you.

Turn to page 23.

"It's you!" comes a faint voice.

You can't believe it. Joy surges through your body. You run to Shining Face and throw your arms around her. "You're alive! But... the others?" Your question is more hopeful than realistic, but if she survived, perhaps the others did too.

"They're all dead," Shining Face says. "I was getting some water when the Turks raided. They didn't see me. I hid in the big rainwater jar."

At that very moment, the Turk who attacked you earlier gallops into the field. He leaps from his horse, confident that neither one of you will try to escape.

"Two for the price of one!" he says. "So much the better. You'll bring good prices in the slave markets of Kashgar, I'm sure of that."

The words slave markets go through you like a knife. You've heard about these places where human beings are sold like animals to serve in the houses of the wealthy, or work in the fields of landlords. People are treated like commodities— no different from gold, silver, leather, tea, silk, or horses.

Turn to the next page.

24

The man turns for a moment to adjust the straps on his horse. You look at Shining Face. You see no fear; her face is a mask of anger and determination.

"The upperhand is on our side," she whispers to you. "We are two; he is but one."

"Yes, but there are the others, too. Don't forget them," you reply, encouraged by her apparent bravery.

"One step at a time," she replies, giving you a smile.

The Turk leaves his horse and approaches the two of you. In his hands are ropes, thick and coarse and blackened from usage. You stand your ground.

"Well, the two of you have a choice. You can come quietly, and I will not tie your hands. Or you can give me trouble, and I will kill one of you immediately, and the other will be tied up like a chicken on its way to the market."

"That isn't a choice," you reply, emboldened by a deep resolve to survive.

"As you like," the Turk says. "One of you will walk, the other will ride. Or one of you could go with my friend, Three Finger Tong. We can wait for him here. He should be back soon."

You turn to Shining Face, but it looks like the decision is yours.

If you decide to walk, turn to page 36.

If you decide to wait for Three Finger Tong and ride with him, turn to page 46.

"Okay, I'll come with you to Luoyang," you say to the couple, your decision a quick one based on an intuitive feeling that these people are kind and will treat you well. If it doesn't work out, you can always leave them.

The rest of the day passes like a holiday. You are free, and you feel important. You are an adult, in charge of your own life, not the property of someone else. What's more, it is obvious to you that these people need you. And they are as new to the city of Luoyang as you are. Together the three of you will discover what it is to live in a glorious city, one fabled throughout the region. The emperor has a palace there, one of many that he owns. There are stories of the many mandarins and landowners who live there in great wealth. As a child you read stories of the court and its elegant men and women, all dressed in silk and wearing jewelry. A whole village could live well for a year with the revenue from one bracelet or necklace.

Turn to the next page.

"Luoyang is a rough place," the man says to you, a note of caution in his voice. His name is Han Yu he tells you, but you can call him Han. His wife is called The Flower on the Water, or Flower for short.

"What do you mean?" you ask. Everything you have ever heard about Luoyang has made it sound like a paradise on earth. On the other hand, people do tend to exaggerate.

Han hesitates for a moment, rearranging the heavy basket he carries. You have already taken his wife's smaller one, while she carries a bag made of beautiful red cloth stuffed with clothes.

Go on to the next page.

"Where there is power and wealth, there is bound to be corruption," Han says. "The Sui emperors brought greatness to China, but with it came greed and treachery. You must be careful in this city. Spies, thieves, and murderers are common. There is intrigue on every corner."

"It's not as bad as Han makes it out," Flower says in a gentle voice. "What he means is that you should not believe everything that you hear, nor trust everyone you meet."

For a fleeting moment you ask yourself whether you have put your trust in this couple too easily. After all, you don't know them, really. But your basic optimism and your ability to judge human nature returns, and you feel confident that this couple is trustworthy.

Turn to the next page.

Three hours later, you are at the River Wei. The crowds there are enormous. There is a holiday atmosphere in the air, with jugglers, musicians, and food vendors selling dried fruit wrapped in paper, gruel in steaming pots, thin pancakes stuffed with meat, and green scallions and a hot sauce. Your eyes are so filled with all the sights that it is difficult for you to take it all in at once.

Suddenly a hush comes over the milling, bustling crowd. It is followed by the blare of horns and the shuffle of drums. The noise grows louder, and you see the first of the warriors on their horses prancing into the flat, earthen area next to the river. The soldiers wear mahogany-colored leather breastplates and arm and shin protectors. They carry lances fluttering with long silk banners of red, yellow, and blue. After the first ten men, there comes a band of thirty or more all armed with bow and arrows, their quivers filled.

Turn to the next page.

"There he is!" shouts a small man dressed in rags. "Look at him! Our leader!"

You stand on the tips of your boots, stretching so that you can see over the heads of the people around you.

Li Shi-min is larger than life. Dressed as a common soldier, he radiates brilliantly. There is a power and a majesty in this man's presence. His eyes sweep the crowd, looking from face to face, making everyone feel important, as if he were singling them out. His horse is the famous Autumn Dew, a large stallion, black as the dark of night, his eyes bright and attentive. The horse seems to reflect the power and quality of its master.

Go on to the next page.

You cannot take your eyes away from this man. He turns to you, and you feel his eyes upon you. He seems to be telling you to join his troops, to become one of his soldiers. Your spirit soars, and then you are reminded of your commitment to Han and Flower. You are torn between staying with them and joining the army of the Great Warrior of China.

If you decide to leave Han and Flower, turn to page 67.

If you decide to stay with your new friends, turn to page 53.

You scramble to your feet, your heart beating loudly, and make a break for freedom. None of the Turks seem to notice, and you are able to make it to safety. You look around, hoping that Li Shi-min and his troops are coming. You stand alone, unharmed, waiting under the morning sun.

Smoke bulges into the sky. The Turks have torched the houses and storage sheds. You know that what they can't carry away with them they burn. The Turks move away from your farm and continue on, toward the neighboring farms. You're safe, at least for the time being.

You check your pocket. Your knife is still there, although it's of little use to you. Speed and cunning are all you can count on now. These men are too strong, too cruel, too practiced in the art of war for you to fight them by hand.

At the edge of the land, you come to an irrigation ditch. It brings water to the farm from a tributary of the River Wei. Most of the time it is dry and useless, which accounts, in part, for the poorness of the land used for farming. There have been times, however, when angry spring rains have filled the stream to the point where it overflowed the banks and ravaged the land. Today it is mostly a muddy trickle.

As you scan the ditch for water to drink, horror overcomes you: you are staring with disbelief at the bodies of your uncle and cousins!

Turn to the next page.

Eyes wild, you slide down the side of the ditch, away from the horror before you, worming your way along for about thirty yards.

You come to a narrow bridge leading to some fields that once belonged to your uncle; now they belong to another, more prosperous farmer. The bridge is seldom used. You crawl underneath it, covering yourself in the shadows with reeds and mud.

If worse comes to worst and you are discovered, you speculate, you hope you will die bravely, honoring your ancestors. Relying on your belief in reincarnation, you promise to return in your next life and seek revenge on the Turks.

Turn to page 57.

The temptation to stay with this nice couple is strong, but there is something inside you that tugs at you to make it on your own. It would be far too easy to take up with the first people that you meet. For a few moments you concentrate on your ancestors, asking your grandfather in particular for help and guidance. His spirit has been a great comfort to you during the last year. You feel that he approves of your decision to continue on to the sacrifice.

The couple decide not to wait for the sacrifice; they want to get to the city of Luoyang as soon as possible.

"Good luck, our friend. May the gods look favorably upon you, and may your days be enriched with good fortune." They make small bows in honor of your spirit; then they are gone, walking confidently toward the city and the new life that awaits them.

Loneliness comes upon you for a moment. You just met these people, you tell yourself. You will meet others. You can always find them in Luoyang, if you need to.

You turn your attention to your journey. Soon you come to a circle where you unexpectedly find Li Shi-min sitting astride his horse, Autumn Dew. You wish with all your might that you were him, and that the crowds gathered were gaping at you with the same wonderment and awe.

Turn to page 47.

Having decided to walk alongside Shining Face and the Turk, you wait while your captor turns his attention to the horizon. His eyes search in a broad sweep. You sense an anxiety in him that suggests fear. These raids by his group and others like him are the thorn of the Chinese people. The Eastern Turks and their ravenous khans have plagued China for more than a hundred years. Emperors have spent fortunes on armies to contain these hordes. The Great Wall itself was built for this purpose, but so far it hasn't been too effective. There is talk that the wall will be extended soon. Rumors, however, have been circulating that political corruption inside the government has led to much unnecessary expense.

According to the elders in the villages and towns, the warlords, the mandarins, and the landowners, those who control thousands of acres of land and many small towns such as yours, are at the root of the troubles.

"We are nothing but slaves to these corrupt officials!" you've heard them say ever since you can remember. "One day, their time will come." It is the hope that the warrior Li Shi-min will be the answer to these problems. Perhaps he will be the savior for all of the people in China, not just the rich.

"Is there a problem?" you dare to ask the Turk.

Go on to the next page.

"There are always problems. Haven't you learned anything in your years? Aagh! What can I get for someone like you? Not much, I'll bet." He spits on the ground, rearranges his belt, and pushes his sword to one side.

"Li Shi-min will get you. Just wait and see," Shining Face says to the Turk defiantly.

Turn to page 40.

"Let's join forces then," you say. "I have no home now thanks to you and those Turks. We can go to Luoyang—join up with Li Shi-min."

"But I'm a Turk. They'd kill me," says Three Finger.

"There are plenty of Turks who have joined the emperor's army. They are called mercenaries, and they work for money. Come, the two of us would make a great team." You are feeling more confident by the minute.

"I don't know," he says. "I'd be a deserter. I shudder to think what the Turks would do if they ever caught me."

After much debate back and forth, you and Three Finger Tong agree to seek out Li Shi-min. Together the two of you head for the city of Luoyang, where you are welcomed into the army of the great hero of China. At last your dream is realized.

The End

"You're a dreamer," the Turk says to Shining Face, lifting her onto his horse. He then jumps up onto the saddle and beckons for you to follow him. "I will ride slowly," he says. "If we are attacked, I will leave you. But don't worry, I will come back with the others. You can swear on your ancestors' graves that I will be back for you, however useless you may be."

"Where are the others?" you ask, trying your best to delay him, hoping Li Shi-min and his troops will find you.

Go on to the next page.

"Get going! Who do you think you are, a teacher? You and your talk." The Turk and Shining Face ride off at a slow trot, and you are forced to run behind them in order to keep up.

"How much farther?" you ask, but you don't have to wait much longer to find out. At the far edge of the field, by the ditch next to the bridge, are two more Turks. One of them has been wounded. He holds his right arm close to his body, and you can see the deep cut through his clothing. Above the wound is a knotted piece of rawhide. A short piece of wood is being used to twist the tourniquet and stop the flow of blood. The man looks pale, pain and fear written all over his face.

Turn to the next page.

"Yi-Tung, we waited for you too long," one of the men says, addressing the Turk. "My brother, he's wounded."

So that's his name—Yi-Tung, you say to yourself. He is famous around these parts. It is said that he once faced Li Shi-min in arm-to-arm combat. But the bravery of the two men was so great, neither one struck a blow, and the fight never took place. The two soldiers stared each other down. Eventually, both men rode off. You could not understand such a fight at the time, and you are not sure that you can understand it any better now.

"The warlord will be here soon, Hungry Eye," Yi-Tung says, ignoring the wounded soldier.

"But what are we to do with these kids? The Chinese will be after us in a flash. We can't take them with us. And what about my brother?"

Go on to the next page.

Yi-Tung looks down upon Hungry Eye, who visibly weakens under the power of his stare. Instinctively you move closer to Yi-Tung, aware to some extent that ultimately he could be your protector. Despite his harsh manner, there is a tone to his voice that leads you to believe he is not all evil.

"Since when do you wish to be chieftain?" Yi-Tung asks Hungry Eye. "Is it that you are braver than me? Stronger, perhaps? Smarter? No, to all of those things. You are greedy and more stupid than you are vicious."

Turn to the next page.

"But how will we get away from Li Shi-min and his men? Look, already they are coming!" Hungry Eye says, pointing to the east.

You can see clouds of dust rising in the late morning sky. It is yellowish and easy to distinguish from the dark, acrid smoke of the burning homes in the village, the charred remains left by the raiders.

Go on to the next page.

"Be quick!" Yi-Tung commands to you. "Hurry, get on Hungry Eye's horse. Now!"

You don't have a chance to delay. Hungry Eye grabs you, swinging you onto the back of the horse. Before you can settle in, the horse is spurred and tears off, Hungry Eye yelling commands for it to go faster. He has been forced to leave his brother behind, and you notice him cast a longing glance over his shoulder, as if to say, I'm sorry, I have no choice.

Yi-Tung and Shining Face are to your right, but you dare not look. It takes all of your strength just to hold on to Hungry Eye and maintain your balance.

Suddenly an idea pops into your head. You could cut the saddle straps with your knife. While Hungry Eye struggles to maintain control, you could jump free of the horse and escape. Your hand eases off Hungry Eye's shirt and clutches the handle of your knife. You feel a sense of power, but you're also fearful. Perhaps this is too dangerous and you should continue to hang on and see what will happen next.

If you decide to cut the saddle straps, turn to page 71.

If you decide to hang on, turn to page 105.

As a prisoner you really don't have much of a choice, even though you decide to wait for Three Finger Tong and ride with him. You hope that Shining Face will be all right.

Looking at the Turk, you wish you were brave enough to stand up to him. What a fine speech you could make. "Who do you think you are?" you would say. You enjoy imagining the way the Turk would look, the surprise and fear on his face when you tell him that you will hound him and his fellow barbarians out of China as far west as the fabled land of Persia, where the Ottoman Turks reign. Then he will know the taste of terror. Those Turks are fiercer than his people, famed for their cruelty. Of course you say nothing as you cover the look of contempt on your face.

"Get going!" the Turk commands. He must be tired, because there isn't as much energy in his voice as there was earlier. There is enough, however, to wake you out of your daydream.

Turn to page 54.

Your thoughts of the sacrifice fade when a soldier makes the following announcement: "By proclamation of the commander of the emperor's troops, Li Shi-min—glorious warrior and lord of this army that protects China from the barbarian hordes—all able-bodied people who wish to join his army will come to the tent set up by the signpost to the city of Luoyang, just beyond the hill," he says pointing.

Heart beating, feet propelling you onward, you rush to the tent. You are not alone, for a great crowd of youths also share your dreams and ambitions. There is much pushing and shoving.

"Hey, watch it, I'm first!" a large man yells to another.

"Who says so?!" replies the other, pushing as hard as he can. "I'm first, and I mean to stay, as the gods are my witness."

"You'll need more than the gods to be a witness for one the likes of you."

Turn to page 49.

With that last comment, the two throw themselves at each other, shouting and screaming vile oath upon vile oath, each questioning the parentage of the other and imploring the gods to bring them victory.

"Look at those fools," says a short, swarthy soldier to his companion, both of whom are grinning. "There'll be plenty of time for fighting where they're going."

"And they'll feed the ravens before the harvest, I'll bet my month's salary on that," says the other as both men laugh.

"Well, let's break it up. We can't have this crowd think we don't believe in discipline."

Turn to the next page.

50

With that, the two soldiers take heavy wooden staves about six feet long and smack both of the combatants across the sides of their heads. The two men fall like sacks of grain.

"Line up! Line up here!" the short soldier shouts to the crowd, which has become quiet and orderly.

You take your place in the long line, not quite as sure as you were before that this is the life for you. By the time you get to the front of the line, almost forty-five minutes later, your resolve has firmed, and you are decidedly ready to be a soldier of the emperor, under the command of the great Li Shi-min.

Go on to the next page.

"Next!" you hear the soldier call out. "Sign here," he says, holding up a long roll of paper with signatures filling the page. You hesitate for a moment, then with courage and hope you affix your signature to the page using a chop, a small wooden peg about the size of your index finger and carved with your personal characters, which you dip in ink. You grandfather made it for you, and you have always carried it with you proudly.

Turn to the next page.

"Listen carefully," a soldier shouts, addressing the new recruits. "You are all soldiers of the emperor. From this day on, you will obey his commands through the Great Warrior Li Shi-min and any and all of his officers and men. Failure to obey is cause for death! Are there any questions?"

There are no questions, and the soldier calls to his comrades, "Take them away!"

The soldiers laugh, looking at the crowd of seventy or so young recruits, of which you are one. "If ten of them see the new year they'll be lucky. The Turks love new flesh," you hear one of them say.

A sudden fear descends upon you like a morning mist, and you wonder if you have made the right decision. Maybe you should desert now, before you get yourself in any deeper. On the other hand, if you stay, you could come to realize your dream and become a hero in the army of Li Shi-min.

If you decide to desert, turn to page 65.

If you decide to stay, turn to page 68.

The temptation is great. This is your dream. This man embodies all of the hope for the future of China. For generations weak emperors squandered the wealth of China. Those days were marked by greed and folly. But this man has destiny in his blood, and the destiny of a greater China in his heart. You want to fight for a better future, but you are sensible and cautious. The rational part of you tugs at you to be more practical. Leaving your impulses aside, at least for the time being, you decide to stay with Han and Flower.

Han gives you a curious yet understanding look. "You'd like to be with him, wouldn't you?" he asks. The look in his eyes tells you that deep down he too would love to join in the fight for freedom.

"Yes, but now is not the time," you say sadly.

"Your time will come," he replies. "Have no fear. I see it written on your face."

You wonder what he means by that. It is reminiscent of what your mother said to you one day before the big illness that took away almost everyone who was dear to you. She too said similar things about you and your future. It made the hair stand up on the back of your head and a shiver run through your body. Talk of the future has always had that effect on you.

Turn to page 59.

For some reason you are not really afraid of this Turk. Granted he is a killer and a thief; however, in the whole scheme of things, his life is nothing but a passing moment. Then again, so is yours. Just as the seasons progress with a preordained certainty, so too will your life progress. You are able to take this man's power over you away by simply disregarding him, by reducing his life proportionately to nothing.

A sense of freedom comes with this realization, the same kind that you have occasionally felt when you and Black Moon sat in the afternoon sun watching a distant point on the horizon, studying the transit of the sun and the movement of the clouds in the sky. Sometimes you have actually felt yourself merging with the earth. Those were wonderful feelings, and you delighted in the knowledge and power of your own personal magnificence.

"Move, I said!" the Turk commands, kicking you in the seat of your pants and sending you flying. The dreamlike moment vanishes in an instant, and the reality of your being a prisoner returns.

"Where am I to wait for Three Finger Tong?" you ask, fear creeping back into your voice, making you a little more cautious. Thoughts about time and your place in the universe are all well and fine, but your life hangs on your actions now, and you need to focus more fully on the moment.

Turn to page 58.

Hours pass, though it seems like days, and you become disoriented and feverish as you lie in the mud, your head filled with the horror of the events of the morning. You had heard stories about these barbarian raids, but the reality is far worse than you had ever imagined.

Finally, at long last, night falls. Slowly you ease your way out of the ditch, your senses alert for any signs of danger. You are thankful for your survival, but the smell of death that pervades the air keeps you humble.

"I will revenge my family!" you decree to the night sky, shaking your first. For now you know that there are more difficult times ahead that you must face.

The End

"I am here," a voice from behind you says. When you turn around, you are surprised to find a boy not much older than you.

"Come, we haven't much time to waste. Get going!" he commands.

"We'll meet back at camp tomorrow, Three Finger," the Turk says. "If you don't show up, we'll be gone, and it will be the worse for you, understand?" The Turk appears anxious to be on his way.

Shining Face looks at you, a mixture of anger and fear on her face. You move over to her quickly, and in a last hug goodbye, you slip her your knife. This is the most you can do for her, and you pray that she will be all right.

"Don't worry, Shining Face, I'll come for you," you announce with as much bravado as you can muster.

"In your next life, maybe," the Turk calls back. Then they are gone, dust kicking up behind the receding figures.

You turn to Three Finger. "Now what?"

"I was going to ask you the same," he replies. "I'm no good at this. I'm no killer. I want out; I've been with these bandits for the last two months, and I can't stand them. My father wanted me to grow up, so he sent me to travel with them. But I've had it up to here." He draws his hand across his throat and then spits.

Turn to page 38.

"So, shall we watch the sacrifice?" Han asks.

"I don't really want to see the white horse killed," you reply.

"Nor do I," he replies. Flower nods her head in agreement.

"But why is it done, Han? I mean, what's a horse got to do with a victory over some stupid barbarians?" you ask, puzzled by the behavior of apparently intelligent people who still carry on what you think are primitive rites.

"It goes back almost two thousand years," Han says, a look of concentration on his face, "when China was but an infant. This yellow soil gives us life. In those days, as now, life centered on the seasons and the crops. If there was rain in the growing time, then the people would prosper. If there was no rain or not enough water, the people would die. We know how to store things better than they did in those early days, but drought can still wipe us out."

"But what does that have to do with killing some poor animal in the name of our battle to stop these Mongolian Turks?" You think you know the answer, but you want to see the way Han thinks.

Turn to the next page.

Han readjusts the belt he wears, puts his hand to his chin, and looks out at the crowd milling around Li Shi-min.

"In those days, a few powerful individuals promised the people that they would protect them, that they would talk to the gods of the earth, sun, and rain in order to assure the harvest. Those people who had the power to talk to the gods became emperors. They offered up gifts to the gods to assure that their wishes for a good harvest would be granted."

Turn to page 62.

"What were these gifts? Were they always animal sacrifices?" you ask.

"No, not always animals," Han replies. "In the beginning they were mostly grain, or fruit. Later, with different emperors, particularly after a rash of terrible harvests where many people died, the sacrifices became animals, sometimes even humans."

This news about human sacrifice has been hinted to you before, but this is the first time you have ever heard it directly stated.

"They really sacrificed human lives?" you ask, appalled. Death by famine, disease, accident, or even in war is understandable, you reason, but the idea of people killing their own in order to bribe the gods is repugnant to you.

"It didn't happen often," Han says, "but in our history there are dark events, just as there are in the history of all peoples. There is that side to human nature that is not understood. We humans seem to have a capacity for cruelty against ourselves that goes beyond anything in the animal kingdom, if you get my meaning."

Go on to the next page.

"I understand," you say. "At least I think I do. But the horse? Why now? Isn't Li Shi-min an intelligent man? Why does he need to sacrifice a horse now? Those days are past. We are a civilized country. We don't need sacrifices, least of all animal sacrifices."

"It's for show. Pure and simple, Li Shi-min is putting on a show for the people. They expect it, and he doesn't want to disappoint them. It will be a great spectacle. Look at the crowd," Han says. "Listen to them. It is what they want."

Turn to the next page.

"But it's not fair," you reply.

"Fairness is a concept, not something that you can eat or plant," Han says. "Right now these people want this sacrifice, and Li Shi-min will give it to them. Fairness is not a concern for them. Do you understand?"

"I think I do, Han. But can't we do something about it?"

"Today? I rather doubt it unless you want to be pulled apart limb from limb by this crowd. They came to see some blood, and it is blood that they will have."

A wild shout goes up, and a surge of energy courses through the crowd like a flash of lightning. A white horse, its head high and its nostrils flaring, prances into the open space by Li Shi-min. It is a beautiful creature, strong, young, and full of spirit.

"They're going to kill him!" you shout in dismay.

"Right you are," a man says, standing next to the three of you. "It will be beautiful! This is a great day," he says, then turns back to the spectacle.

"We needn't stay," Han says. "We can continue on to Luoyang."

You nod, but something tugs at you to stay. Han and Flower wait for your decision.

If you decide to leave and go to Luoyang, turn to page 79.

If you decide to stay and watch the sacrifice, turn to page 89.

Cautiously, you move to the rear of the crowd, watching the troopers, and waiting for your chance to escape. The crowd shuffles past, some of them quite happy with themselves, others more subdued as they imagine the enormity of their decision.

"Hurry up! We haven't got all day. Form two lines. Quick!" comes an order.

The crowd mills forward as the troopers move in with short sticks, herding you into lines like cattle. You fall behind, crouching next to a clump of bushes over by three mulberry trees. The soldiers march off, the troopers setting a cadence and prodding the lines forward with the short sticks.

Turn to page 85.

As if by a powerful magnet, you are drawn to Li Shi-min and his army. Without so much as a goodbye to your two new friends, Han and Flower, you slip off into the crowd and edge closer to the spot where Li Shi-min rests astride his horse.

The crowd pushes, squeezing against one another in an attempt to get closer to the warrior hero of China. His soldiers, each one handpicked to serve as his special guard, surround Li Shi-min like a human fence, keeping the crowd back. You squirm and twist until you are up against two of the soldiers. They look down at you, their eyes haughty and proud. Each one is over six feet tall. You know they are trained to give their lives for Li Shi-min's defense, without so much as a moment's hesitation. They are assured their rightful place with their ancestors if their service is done with bravery and merit.

"Please, let me through," you beg.

"Do you wish to be a sacrifice too?" the soldier in front of you asks sarcastically. He pushes you back with his round shield, but you manage to duck underneath it, squiggling between him and the other soldier.

You've made it—you are inside the circle, facing the mighty Li Shi-min. The crowd senses a change and roars its approval at you for your bravery. You are momentarily frozen to the spot, unsure of what to do next. The circle widens for a moment, and two guards from the opposite side point at you, yelling a warning.

Turn to page 87.

68

You decide to stay with the army. Three months later, you are a trained soldier of the emperor, proudly wearing the breastplate and forearm and leg armor of a foot soldier. It is a bright day, the temperature perfect for marching. The sun is warming the air, your body feels good, hardened by the training, and your mind is alert, your spirit ready for action.

You are part of an advanced column marching after the Turks beyond the Great Wall and into the plains of Outer Mongolia. So far you haven't come upon any Turks, except for the occasional skeleton marking the spot of a previous battle or encounter.

Turn to page 88.

Hungry Eye shouts, whipping the horse to go faster. The animal immediately responds with a burst of speed that almost throws you off its back. You clench the belly of the horse with your legs and utter a short prayer for help. You're not sure which is worse, being thrown off this wild horse at full speed, or being the prisoner of these Eastern Turks, who will surely sell you into slavery in the vast markets of Kashgar at the western end of the great Gobi Desert.

There is no time to think. Yi-Tung and Hungry Eye are outrunning the soldiers of Li Shi-min. You wonder what Shining Face is thinking as you prepare for action. The knife blade in your hand finds the leather harness, and you begin a sawing motion. You find it difficult because the horse is jerking as it hurtles across fields, some newly tilled, others rough stubble from the previous season. There are irrigation ditches and low walls—all in all a dangerous ride.

The knife accidentally slices into the flesh of the horse, who momentarily bucks; Hungry Eye gains control and spurs it onward.

"Now!" you think to yourself. With all your might you finish cutting through the saddle straps and launch yourself off the back of the horse. You hit the yellow earth soundly and roll, your arms and legs akimbo. You feel a pain in your arm, but you have no time to worry about that now.

Turn to the next page.

The horse bucks from the sudden movement, and you watch as Hungry Eye is thrown violently from the horse and lands facedown in the dirt. His body is lifeless, and you know that he will no longer be a problem for you.

You look around for Shining Face. Yi-Tung has not stopped, you realize, but you are not surprised. Your heart fills with sadness for Shining Face. Then the pain from your arm hits you fully, and you pass out.

Go on to the next page.

When you regain consciousness, there is a stillness in the air that startles you. Gone are the shouts and screams and the sound of hooves. Gone too is the smoke. The fires must have burned themselves out, and the afternoon breeze seems to have dissipated the ugly black clouds that were once houses and storage for food.

For a moment you think that the events of the morning were only a nightmare. But then your eye spots the body of Hungry Eye and the reality hits you. A wave of nausea overcomes you, mingled with the throbbing pain of your arm. You turn onto your side and cover your head with your arms, but there are no tears. You used them all up when your parents died; when you left home for your uncle's farm; when you felt alone even in the midst of a large second family. You realize you must survive. Now is the time for you to build a new life for yourself, one that is yours and yours alone.

Turn to the next page.

Suddenly you hear a noise. You look around you as it grows louder. It's coming from Hungry Eye, you realize. He's still alive!

Scrambling to your feet and ignoring the pain in your arm for the moment, you move to Hungry Eye, roll him over, and examine him.

"What are you, the devil?" he screeches at you as you slowly move his head. You are amazed that his neck is not broken; it certainly looked like it was at first. This Eastern Mongolian Turk is stronger than you imagined. He would have to be, you reason, in order to survive the life of a warring nomad.

"I'm trying to help you," you reply.

"I need some water," he says, without a trace of thankfulness in his voice.

"The horse has run off. There is no water around here. How badly are you hurt?" you ask. Suddenly the pain in your arm returns with great intensity. You try your best to conceal it, but your face gives you away.

"So, you too have received a present from the gods. They send them just to remind us who's in charge. Is it bad?"

"Bad enough," you reply.

Turn to page 76.

"Do you know of any people around here who would take us in?" Hungry Eye asks. You are shocked that he would even ask such a question after the raid this morning.

"There are farms not too far away," you reply, "but they may have been attacked. You would not be too welcome there, I am sure."

Feeling more courageous since this man is wounded and now less of a threat, you wish Li Shi-min and his warriors would arrive. Then a terrible thought enters your mind. Suppose the dust cloud you saw was not Li Shi-min and his men at all. Suppose they were more Turks, off on another raid, returning to Yi-Tung. What if you are all alone with this wounded Turk when they return?

"Well, we can't just stay here all day and be food for the buzzards," Hungry Eye says. "This calls for—"

"Where does it hurt?" you ask, forgetting your own pain for the moment. Maybe your arm isn't broken. Perhaps it is just sprained.

"Where doesn't it hurt, is more like it. What happened, anyway?"

You are tempted to tell him the truth, but you think better of it.

Go on to the next page.

"The horse stumbled and fell," you tell him.

"We need help," Hungry Eye states directly. "What can you do?"

The farm of Singing Tree is nearby. You could get help for the two of you there. But after the events of the morning, you think twice. Maybe you should just leave Hungry Eye to suffer—just as your family suffered at the hands of him and the Turks—and seek help for yourself.

If you decide to get help from the farm of Singing Tree, turn to page 93.

If you decide to leave Hungry Eye and take care of yourself, turn to page 101.

You cannot bear to stay and watch the sacrifice. You decide to leave, but it is difficult to make your way through the crowd. You fear being separated from Han and Flower. A burly youth, a few years older than you are, bumps into you.

"Running dog of the foul barbarians, out of my way!" he curses, pushing past you. Instinctively you reach into your pocket to see if the small cloth sack that holds your coins is still there. It is not!

"Stop him!" you scream, anger rising in you like a river in flood. "Stop him. He's a thief!" You struggle against the crowd, trying to chase the youth, but the crowd doesn't hear you, or if it does, it doesn't care.

Desperately you fight against the tide. You finally break free, but the youth is gone, vanished into the crowd. Filled with anger and despair, you turn to Han and Flower, who have followed you through the moving mass.

Turn to the next page.

"Lose much?" Han asks, a look of concern on his face.

"Yes and no," you reply. "It's all I have, so it's a lot to me, but it was so little that it hardly counts." In a strange way you feel enormously free at this moment. You have nothing but your ambition and your desire. You also have your new friends and the prospect of work with them.

"Well, don't worry. You are working with us, and we have money. Again, like you it isn't a fortune, but it's a start. Come, let's hurry. The city isn't far. We can see the walls from that little hill over there." He points to the gently rising land and the road that snakes toward it. Your spirit soars, and you are glad to get away from the crowd and the sacrifice.

Go on to the next page.

Flower has listened to the conversation, but she has said nothing until now. "What is your name?" she asks. "Here we are, we have gone on and on about ourselves all this time, and we don't even know your name."

For a moment you hesitate. After all, this is a brand new beginning for you. Suddenly an idea flashes into your mind. Why not create a new name for your new life? Out with the old and in with the new. You momentarily reflect, consulting your ancestors, asking their permission for the change. It is a dramatic thing to do, and you do not wish to offend them.

"I wish to have a new name," you tell them. A look of surprise washes across both their faces, and then Han grins and replies, "Great idea! I like your spirit. Let us help."

"I kind of like the name New Moon. What do you think?"

"Well it's a good start, but you don't look like a new moon to me," Flower says, giggling. "How about something like Moving Dawn?"

"Uhhh, well..." you reply, studying the ground at your feet. You don't like that name at all.

"It's a personal choice," Han interrupts.

Turn to page 83.

"I think I'd like to be called Birch. It is simple, easy to remember, and I like birch trees."

"Done!" they say in unison, clapping you on the back.

"Let's get going, Birch."

"I'm ready," you reply, having a taste of your new name and liking it already.

Turn to the next page.

Just then a roar goes up from the crowd. The three of you turn around. You are about a hundred yards away, and the noise is so loud that it is hard to hear yourself speak. Then, as quickly as it started, the shouts die down. Silence follows—a silence filled with an eerie sense of anticipation.

Suddenly a horrible scream pierces the air. You don't have to ask what it is. It is the sacrifice—the sound of the white horse. The crowd roars once again, the tone changed to one of approval, husky and excited, as if wanting more.

"Let's get out of here," Han says.

Together the three of you hurry toward the city of Luoyang, whose brown outer walls you can just make out over the hill. Your new life is just beginning, filled with images of events both good and bad, right and wrong. "It is as it should be," you say to yourself. "It is the way life is. It is time now for me to make my own way, on the path that leads toward that which is good and right for me."

The End

"What do you think you're doing?" asks a voice, taking you off guard. You feel yourself freeze, unable to move, let alone speak.

"Well, haven't you a tongue?"

"I'm—well, I'm—" you mumble, looking up. You find yourself staring at an old man with white hair and a thin wispy beard. He looks important, but he is dressed like a beggar. One of his arms is missing, and the sleeve of his jacket is pinned to the shoulder.

"You're trying to get away from the army, aren't you?"

"Yes sir," you answer, deciding that it is better to tell the truth rather than deny it.

Turn to the next page.

"Well, you're less of a fool than I took you for. See this?" the old man asks, gripping his empty sleeve with his other hand.

You nod, fascinated by the man and his missing arm.

"Taken by an Orkhon Turk up by Kashgar. It's not worth it, my young friend."

"You mean you were one of them?" you ask, pointing to the receding line of new recruits.

"One of them, indeed," he replies. "I was a sergeant major for eleven years. And I loved it for all of those years, but then—this arm and fifteen good friends and comrades, all gone. Looking back, it still makes no sense. Some may enjoy the killing, but not me. You want my advice, be a farmer and stay away from the army."

"But how do I get away?"

"It seems to me that you are already away. Come, help an old cripple carry his bundle to Luoyang. You'll be safe, as safe as anyone can be in these times of ours."

You are thankful beyond belief for this second chance. When you arrive in Luoyang, you plan to look for the nice couple you met on your way to the sacrifice. You only hope they remember you, and that your uncle, and the army of Li Shi-min, never find you.

The End

At that moment Li Shi-min takes notice of you and beckons you to his side. As if in a dream, you move toward the Great Warrior. You seem to have no control over your actions.

"Why are you here?" Li Shi-min asks you firmly, without a trace of any hostility.

"It is my destiny, my lord. I am to join you, to be one of your warriors."

"Who told you this?"

"No one, my lord. It is something I have felt for a long time."

"Let me see your hand," Li Shi-min commands.

You lift it up, and he examines the lines on your palm. Then he motions to one of his men.

"Take this young soldier. The future lies with the likes of youth like this."

In a daze, you are led away to begin your new life. You begin to reflect upon what a day this has been for you, but all you care about now is your future.

The End

88

Before you know what is happening, an arrow enters your chest, and with it your life rushes out. The next thing you know, you are being welcomed by your ancestors. Your parents and grandfather greet you with open arms.

"Never even saw him, did you?" your father says.

"No. What happened?" you ask.

"It doesn't really matter," he replies. "You are one of us now."

The End

The mood of the crowd captures you, and you decide to stay and watch the sacrifice. It is almost hypnotic. A noise and a vibration comes from the crowd. You feel yourself caught up in its swell, buffeted, twisted, and fascinated by the energy of the moment.

"Han?" you cry out, but he and Flower are nowhere to be seen. It is as if they never were, as if the time spent with them was nothing more than a dream. "Han! Flower!" you cry out again. But still you have no response.

You push against the crowd, but it is like a solid wall, alive and breathing, moving and chanting. You feel as though your very breath is being squeezed out of you. There is no room for movement.

Horns sound out a blast, and suddenly the crowd stops. The notes drift out into the air like a memory. All is silent.

Your eyes are drawn to the space beyond the people and the river. The white horse, sensing that something is about to happen, paws the ground, its eyes darting from face to face. You know that it is ready to bolt, to flee this horrid place and what is about to happen.

"No!" you cry out. Your voice carries through the air, clear and resonant, breaking the silence. Li Shi-min turns to you, his face animated with question and curiosity.

The words, "Let him go!" erupt from your throat; you are no longer consciously in control of yourself and your actions.

Turn to the next page.

The crowd gasps at your effrontery. An island of space appears around you. You step forward, propelled by an inner force. Slowly, you walk toward Li Shi-min. You are not aware of the crowd—only of the Great Warrior himself and the white horse. Everything else has vanished from your sight.

"What is it you want?" Li Shi-min asks. His voice is calm, his tone firm and normal. He waits, studying your face as one would the sunset, with patience, pleasure, and anticipation.

Turn to page 92.

"It is within your power to save life, not take it," you begin, not knowing where the words are coming from. "It is enough to have the people gathered here. Sacrifice the spectacle."

Li Shi-min nods his head slowly, then looks at the crowd. He says, "We are all protectors of life and of China; we are not killers and murderers. The horse shall live as a symbol to all."

There is a tense moment when the crowd, robbed of its pleasure, is uncertain of its response. It wavers like a headless dragon, not knowing which way to turn. Then a group begins to cheer. Several more join in. Finally all of the crowd is roaring its approval.

"The horse shall live! All hail Li Shi-min!"

You melt into the crowd, searching for your friends, Han and Flower. When you find them, they nod their approval, as pleased to have met you as you are to have met them.

The End

"There is a farm nearby called Singing Tree. It is not far. Will you be all right here by yourself?" you ask Hungry Eye.

"I don't have much of a choice. I can't move without help. I will wait for you to return."

You try to make him as comfortable as you can. Wounded as he is, you now see him in a different light. Strange, you think, how one moment you can feel one way and completely opposite the next. Your mind races back to the events of the morning. Sometimes you surprise yourself with the conflicting feelings that live inside you.

"I'll leave now. It will take me almost two hours, maybe even more. I can't guarantee that they will treat you with kindness. They might not let me return for you. They may even kill you."

"The will of God, then. If I'm left here to die, as I have left my brother, I won't blame you. You owe me nothing. I myself have rarely given mercy; I don't expect it in return."

"I'll come back. I promise."

Turn to the next page.

94

Your arm still hurts, but it does not appear to be broken. In time, this pain too will heal.

The way to the farm of Singing Tree is not difficult to find, and you set off in its direction. The sun is now past its zenith, and its warmth is comforting. Peace has returned to your part of the earth, at least momentarily. You think of your ancestors, watching your every move, hearing your every thought, knowing your every desire. With life comes great responsibility, you realize.

Go on to the next page.

Turning around, you look back at Hungry Eye, lying on the ground in pain and uncertainty. You feel a oneness with him, and it feels strange. Perhaps it is because you are both outcasts. You too have felt isolated, wounded, abandoned, and alone. Your wounds might not have been physical ones, but they hurt just the same. Sadness and remorse weigh heavily upon you. But as your grandfather used to say, "Do not welcome self-pity. It is but a poor guest who will rob you of much joy and energy."

You remember the old man fondly. He had such dignity and wisdom. For as long as you knew him he was the unofficial headman in the village. People went to him with their problems and consulted him for advice. It is said that you are very much like him. You wonder if this is true. As you walk, you find that you miss him more than ever.

Turn to page 97.

The path to Singing Tree turns out to be longer than you remembered. Hunger and thirst follow you, and your feet feel heavy and awkward. Stopping for a moment, you scan the horizon on the off chance that there are soldiers there. But there is nothing; only a flock of blackbirds turning in the air.

The land rises sharply, and from the crest of the rise you can see the farm. It looks to be in good shape, untouched by the Turks. There is no damage, no burning, no death here. Two people are out working in the fields, and a dog lazes in the sun by the doorway. A trickle of smoke climbs into the sky from a cooking fire. Everything is as it should be.

Turn to the next page.

98

You run down to the farm, calling to them out loud.

"What is it?" the farmer asks. He is a young man with a wife and two small children. He is a hard worker, proud of his farm and his family.

"Turks! They burned our farm!" The horror of the memory rushes back to you, and for the moment you forget the Turk called Hungry Eye lying on the ground several miles in the distance. Slowly you recount to the farmer all the painful details of your day.

"Shining Face is with them. They've got her. She'll be sold as a slave!" How could you allow yourself to have forgotten her, you wonder.

"We'll see about that," the farmer says. "We've had enough of these barbarians! It is time for the Chinese Dragons to rid China of these horrible wolves! I will go to Luoyang. I will implore Li Shi-min to chase these bandits and murderers to the four corners of China and kill them all. He will bring back Shining Face. You will see."

These are good, strong words, you think, but you have heard them from others before, and still the Turks come with their raids. But the mention of the Chinese Dragons brings hope; they are spirits of good, of life, of fertility. They bring the rains that mean growth. They stand against evil.

"Come with me. You can tell your story directly to the Great Warrior. He will listen to you. He does not forget his people. Come, we will go now."

Go on to the next page.

"But there is a man. He is wounded and needs our help," you say, pointing in the direction you have come.

"Who is this man?" the farmer asks.

You stall for time, trying to think of a reply. "He is badly hurt."

The farmer is a shrewd man, and he squints at you for a moment. "You're not telling me everything. Is he one of them?"

"Yes. Yes, he is. But he is hurt. He needs our help," you repeat.

"Would he show mercy to our people?" the farmer asks. "Did he show mercy to your family?"

"That is not the issue here. We are not barbarians. We can show mercy, it does not cost us anything." For a moment you examine what you are saying. It is your grandfather speaking through you, you realize.

Turn to the next page.

100

The farmer fixes his stare on you, then nods his head slowly.

"You speak with wisdom. You are right, to give mercy is a great act. To withhold it is a sin against our ancestors. First to this man, then to Li Shi-min."

With the knowledge in your heart that you are doing the right thing, you lead the farmer to the wounded Turk called Hungry Eye. When you reach him, you find that he is dead. You have no time to consider the wheels of justice. You are off to see Li Shi-min and to find Shining Face.

The End

A hardness comes over you as you look at this man. For you he embodies all that is evil in the world. He is harsh and cruel; a killer of men, women, and children. He has no respect for life or property. But now that he is injured, he hopes for treatment that he probably wouldn't give to you if the situation were reversed. You don't know this for a fact. But it is something you feel from within.

You let your mind drift back to the events of the morning—the screams, the burning of the farm, the bodies of your family. This person is your enemy. What is it to you if he dies? It is his bad luck, you reason. This harsh feeling is uncommon for you, but you can't forget the terror you felt, or the pain your family suffered.

Turn to the next page.

102

With a heavy heart you turn your back on Hungry Eye. Despite his protests, you start out to find the Great Warrior, Li Shi-min. It has been decided now—you will join his forces in any capacity you can. If they won't have you as a soldier, then you will become a cook, or a servant, whatever they wish, just as long as you can serve.

You stride along, the pain in your arm less severe now that you have made up your mind. Tugging at your heart is the image of Hungry Eye, lying wounded and defenseless under the sun. You promise yourself that the first person you see you will tell about the Turk. Let them decide what to do with him. If his severed head ends up on a stake outside the walls of Luoyang, then so be it. That is his fortune. The decision is no longer yours.

For now you must move forward, toward the promise of the future.

The End

You hang on as tight as you can. The ride is furious, and you expect to be thrown from the back of the horse and tossed to the ground like a bag of grain. Hungry Eye whips the horse and kicks him in the ribs, urging him ever faster and faster. You steal an occasional glimpse at Yi-Tung and Shining Face; they too are riding at full speed.

Hungry Eye approaches a low wall. As the horse bolts over it, his rear hooves catch the top. For a moment the animal falters, almost toppling over. Then it straightens, and once again you are flying across the fields. A sense of exhilaration as well as terror overcome you on your wild flight. For just a moment you imagine what the life of the Eastern Turks must be like. You imagine the fires at night under the vast Mongolian sky. You see the felt tents. You hear the talk, the sound of songs, the smell of stews bubbling in big iron pots, and the pleasant aroma of tea.

For a moment you almost wish that you were a nomad on the great steppes and plains, living a life of wandering. You want no part of the raiding and the fighting, but the idea of living on the move excites you.

The ride seems to last forever. Now and again Hungry Eye looks over his shoulder to see if Li Shi-min and his warriors are coming. On his face is a demented grin of delight. You are frightened by this man.

Turn to the next page.

106

The sun begins to shift slowly in the late afternoon sky. Thirst, hunger, and fatigue overwhelm you. When will this mad ride stop? Granted, the horse is no longer roaring along at top speed, but holding on has taken a lot out of you.

You look for Yi-Tung and Shining Face, but they are nowhere to be seen. Fear overwhelms you like a sudden chill. You are all alone with this Turk, far from help. You wish the good spirits of the Chinese Dragons could help you now.

As you ride you notice a passing farm. Then another. You pass several small houses and shops. Suddenly you recognize the area. You are not far from the town where you were born. In one afternoon the Turk has covered the same distance that took you several days to walk.

Pulling his shirt and leather vest, you ask, "Why not stop here? We can get food and drink, perhaps even a place to rest for the night."

"Do you take me for a fool? Surely I will be captured, and my fine head will end up on a sharp stake outside the village for the crows and ravens to peck at. But then, that is your plan, isn't it?"

Despite his words, Hungry Eye slows the horse down to a walk. You see him sweep his head back and forth, checking the area for safety. Oddly enough, there are no people to be seen. The village seems deserted. The villagers must have heard of the Turkish raids and gone to seek refuge in the great city of Luoyang.

Go on to the next page.

Your body aches from the ride, and your throat is as dry as grain. You think of the events of the day. The Eastern Turks are a plague on the land. But this sort of brutality has been around for hundreds of years.

The history of China itself is one of much war and suffering. In the past, emperors delighted in sending out military expeditions against other Chinese in order to subdue them and enforce their rule. The commanders of these expeditions gained great merit for the victories, and they were judged by the number of heads severed and piled high for the emperor to see.

Turn to the next page.

108

"Maybe we should stop and rest," Hungry Eye admits. "But just for a minute, mind you. No tricks, or it will be your head and not mine feeding the birds!" Hungry Eye brings the horse to a halt and leaps to the ground.

Your legs feel weak and wobbly as you dismount and walk toward the nearest house. Your village is about two miles beyond.

"Anyone here?" you cry out, standing in front of the humble earthen house.

Your call is met by silence. Then you see a movement inside. "We mean no harm," you say.

An aged woman, her face lined with wrinkles, comes to the door. "They're all gone," she croaks.

Turn to page 110.

"Where have they gone?" you ask the old woman.

"To the next village...for a meeting," she replies coldly.

"What for?" you ask.

She points to the tree where Hungry Eye is standing, then spits on the ground with hatred and disgust.

"Why are you still here?" you query.

"Death means little to me. I welcome it like a long nap after a good meal."

"You mean you expect to be killed by the Turks?"

"I expect nothing. I can see you have much to learn. Li Shi-min and his soldiers are in the village. I suggest you save your questions for him." With that she spits on the ground once again, then turns around and vanishes inside her house.

Go on to the next page.

"What did she say?" Hungry Eye asks.

"Li Shi-min is in the next town," you blurt out, not quite sure why you have told this Turk the truth. At any rate it has its effect. You see fear on Hungry Eye's face.

"How far?" he says, his eyes wide with fear.

"Less than a mile," you reply. A sudden rush of hope surges through you. Li Shi-min is near, and he will save you. You can feel it in your bones. "He will be here any moment," you add, delighting in the apprehension you see etched in Hungry Eye's face.

You wish that Black Moon were with you now. The very thought of your dog and what happened to him brings a wave of hatred over you. It cleanses your senses, and you imagine yourself growing to an immense size, becoming more and more powerful by the minute, capable of anything.

"I will kill him!" Hungry Eye shouts, pounding his palm with his fist. "The gods have given me this moment! Praise be to them for this opportunity!"

Turn to the next page.

112

Your anger quickly vanishes, replaced by fear. Once again you are humbled. *What have I gotten myself into now?* you ask yourself. I should have said nothing. Sometimes you think that there are several people inside you; one brave, one cowardly; one intelligent, and another who is a fool. You don't seem to be able to control which one it is who takes command of the situation. Once again you learn your lesson too late.

"Death to Li Shi-min!" Hungry Eye shouts. "I will send him marching—back to his ancestors." He stomps around, looking like a rooster in a farmyard, all puffed up and proud of himself. "And you—you will be the one who causes his death." A smile spreads across his weathered, bearded face.

A resolve builds up deep within you to conquer this man and others like him. You will save Li Shi-min. You will gain recognition, fame. You will realize your dream—you will serve in the army of Li Shi-min!

But first things first. You have to take care of Hungry Eye. But how? You could attack him, hoping to catch him off guard. But perhaps you should wait things out, develop a strategy as events unfold.

If you attack Hungry Eye, turn to page 118.

If you wait and see what his plans are, turn to page 113.

You decide to wait and see what Hungry Eye's plans are before you make a move.

"You will be the bait!" he says, ranting. "The Great Warrior will come to save you, but I'll get him! It will be simple, quick. Then I will be khan and emperor of all China!" Hungry Eye is starting to get swept away by his delusions of grandeur.

Hungry Eye hatches a plan and wastes no time putting it into effect. He will lure Li Shi-min here by sending the old woman with a message: He is willing to negotiate a treaty of peace. As an offering, he will turn you over. But he will only do this with Li Shi-min personally.

Turn to page 115.

Hungry Eye knows that Li Shi-min is brave, perhaps foolishly brave. Two hours later Li Shi-min proves him right. The Great Warrior, with six of his soldiers, approaches the town, riding into the trap!

Li Shi-min rides his brilliant black charger—the one he calls Autumn Dew. He wears a breastplate of hardened leather and his helmet shines. His lance is held high, a streaming golden silk banner on its end. Beside him his soldiers ride strong mounts that snort and paw the earth with their powerful hooves.

Hungry Eye is on his horse. It looks rough and ugly in comparison to Autumn Dew. Slowly he advances, his short sword held at his side, as he approaches Li Shi-min.

Turn to the next page.

116

You walk beside Hungry Eye, your wrists tied to him by a leather thong. Tension builds within you.

Li Shi-min, stern faced, advances slowly. He stops and lifts his hand when suddenly Hungry Eye raises his sword. You yank him sideways with a powerful pull of the thong around your wrist. Both of you crash to the ground.

Li Shi-min's warriors instantly surround Hungry Eye, tie him up, then unbind you.

"My Lord!" you cry. "He meant to kill you!"

"I know," says a voice from beside the house. A tall man clad in a commander's garb steps out— this is the real Li Shi-min!

"Trust must be earned, not given easily like a drink of water," he says, smiling at you. "This Turk is not to be trusted." He looks at Hungry Eye. "But you are brave. I would like you to come with me, join me and my men. We can use a soldier like you."

Turn to page 119.

Hoping to catch Hungry Eye off guard, you rush toward him, a scream starting deep within you and erupting like a torrent. Your knife is held high, the sun streaking off its slender blade.

A vicious blow stops you, catching you on the side of the head. You spin downward, a spiral of lights floating out from within you, up toward the far reaches of the universe.

From above you see the Great Wall of China. It looks like a dragon, curling its way over the rich Chinese land—a dragon that brings rain and rebirth to all.

In a momentary flash you find yourself on a giant mountaintop. Before you stand your ancestors, welcoming you to your final resting place. As nice as it appears to be, you wish you were alive, back home on your farm.

The End

You are overwhelmed with a feeling of pride and joy. The day has been long and difficult for you, and there has been much pain and sorrow. You will be only too happy to join Li Shi-min and his army. Now is your chance to prove yourself and to serve your country by helping to defeat the Turks.

The End

ABOUT THE ARTISTS

Illustrator: Vladimir Semionov was born in August 1964 in the Republic of Moldavia, of the former USSR. He is a graduate of the Fine Arts Collegium in Kishinev, Moldavia, as well as the Fine Arts Academy of Romania, where he majored in graphics and painting, respectively. He has had exhibitions all over the world, in places like Japan and Switzerland, and is currently Art Director of the SEM&BL Animacompany animation studio in Bucharest.

Cover Artist: Jintanan Donploypetch. Jintanan was born on September 1981 in Nakorn Pathom, Thailand and has just graduated from Faculty of Decorative Arts, Silpakorn University. During her studies, she collected numerous awards including "Best Animation" from the Thailand Animation Association. She has worked as an Art Designer at Kantana Animation House and is now an Artist at Tajkanit Partnership.

ABOUT THE AUTHOR

R. A. Montgomery attended Hopkins Grammar School, Williston-Northampton School and Williams College where he graduated in 1958. Montgomery was an adventurer all his life, climbing mountains in the Himalaya, skiing throughout Europe, and scuba-diving wherever he could. His interests included education, macro-economics, geo-politics, mythology, history, mystery novels, and music. He wrote his first interactive book, *Journey Under the Sea*, in 1976 and published it under the series name *The Adventures of You*. A few years later Bantam Books bought this book and gave Montgomery a contract for five more, to inaugurate their new children's publishing division. Bantam renamed the series *Choose Your Own Adventure* and a publishing phenomenon was born. The series has sold more than 260 million copies in over 40 languages.

For games, activities, and other fun stuff, or to write to Chooseco, visit us online at CYOA.com

THE ABOMINABLE SNOWMAN

CHOOSE FROM 28 ENDINGS!

BY R. A. MONTGOMERY

JOURNEY
UNDER THE SEA

CHOOSE FROM 42 ENDINGS

BY R. A. MONTGOMERY

SPACE AND BEYOND

CHOOSE FROM 42 ENDINGS

BY R. A. MONTGOMERY

THE LOST JEWELS OF NABOOTI

BY R. A. MONTGOMERY

MYSTERY OF THE MAYA

CHOOSE FROM 39 ENDINGS!

BY R. A. MONTGOMERY

HOUSE OF DANGER

BY R. A. MONTGOMERY

RACE FOREVER

CHOOSE FROM 33 ENDINGS!

BY R. A. MONTGOMERY

ESCAPE

CHOOSE FROM 27 ENDINGS

BY R. A. MONTGOMERY

TROUBLE ON PLANET EARTH

CHOOSE
FROM 22
ENDINGS!

BY R. A. MONTGOMERY

CHOOSE YOUR OWN ADVENTURE® 12

WAR WITH THE EVIL POWER MASTER

CHOOSE FROM 30 ENDINGS!

BY R. A. MONTGOMERY

CUP OF DEATH

CHOOSE FROM 23 ENDINGS!

BY SHANNON GILLIGAN